In Autumn

In Autumn

By: Eric Weiss

iUniverse, Inc.
New York   Bloomington

In Autumn

iUniverse books may be ordered through booksellers or by contacting:

iUniverse
1663 Liberty Drive
Bloomington, IN 47403
www.iuniverse.com
1-800-Authors (1-800-288-4677)

ISBN: 978-1-4401-6829-1 (sc)
ISBN: 978-1-4401-6831-4 (ebook)

Printed in the United States of America

iUniverse rev. date: 10/2/2009

ONE

Tracks of a Train

I've never seen a train
On these tracks

Moving forward
Or coming back,

Past the dead-end docks
Of the steel mill,

Through
The tunnel of trees,

Over the bridge
Of our man-made sea.

Sometimes at night,
I wake, swearing to have heard

A long hollow
Whistle

But coming to the tracks
The morning after,

I find the penny
I placed on the rail

Still lying there,
Firmly pressed from the mint

And not from
The weight of moving freight.

Detour

How on earth did the tractor trailer
End up on its back like a bug,

Legs moving,
But not knowing how to turn over,

Surrounded by flashing lights
Of the emergency crew and their crane?

Traffic detoured from the highway,
To the back roads of a rural town,

Full of hollow factories
And the plump woman

In a sundress that shows the red shadow
Of yesterday's tank top,

Talking to kids on bikes
They are much too large for.

The library,
Bank,

And medical center,
Are all closed.

But Dairy Queen is open
And the gas station too,

As we parade through,
Like visitors at the zoo.

Down a Rural Road

Down a rural road,
Watching the sun's rays rising

Through the skeleton
Of an emaciated barn:

The steaming thaw
Of frozen fields,

Frayed stripes of an American flag,
Whipping in the wind.

A few cows,
A random house,

A distant billboard announces
A new golf course.

Rambling

I am a rambler of roads,
Though I could find good land
      I suppose.

But manor's not for me.

No, intrigue carries me
Far beyond the eye's distance,
Into the great imagination
Of that far-off destination.

Yes
      That is I

Floating on by,
Carried by the wind,
      The waves,
Crossing roads,
Sleeping naked to the sky,
Saturating myself
With the clouds' emptiness.

I meet many names
And sing their songs.
Time is never too long,
And a journey is nothing in itself
But the spirit of the heart's beat
With the notes of the people's places.

So when asked who I am,
"I am but a shadow," is my reply.
For who am I to deny
Them the right to know
The essence of their luminescent glow.

Man Made Full

A Constant Yesterday

The last line
To a poem
Sitting on the window sill.

Dirty paw prints from the cat
And dead flies lay upon it.

They sought an escape
But their wings hit the window
And instead landed silently on words.

Now we clean his house,
His things left as if he were
In the other room smoking his pipe
While listening to a ballgame on the radio.

He never spoke of poems,
The stoic old man.

He just left them nameless
In random places.

Little treasures,
He always had,
      Secret pleasures.

Surrendered now,
In the slanted rays of the autumn sun
And the anguish of family
Digging through a life, still breathing.

Porch

The grasshopper on the spindle,
Sideways upright,
Sky lowering into night.

Tea sipping,
Rocking in my chair,
Letting go of any cares.

Chores to be done
And some completed,
However temporary.

A tree sways in the still woods.
It tries hard to rain,
But my hands can't squeeze the clouds.

I've met nights like this before;
An old friend,
This dark has come again,

To rekindle and ignite my past
But not all is worth the work;
Re-creation is no recreation.

Gazing into the open field I see
Disappearing lights of ghostly glares;
Cars share their fabricated stares.

I have shared my stares through the years
However unwarranted,
They were innocent in perspective.

But nothing can be seen
To the direction of my vision,
I am invisible.

On the porch rocking in my chair,
Offering my blood to the bugs,
Who drink till drunk.

And I will arise
To express my luck,
Cursing in scratching fit
That I was too melancholy
To move out of the bug's dark world
But rather dawdled

In the parameters
Of the infinite,
Stretching to reach

Nothing evident,
But something sensed
In the need to achieve

A great enlightened state,
So as to make my earth shake
And take away anxiety's weight,

Compressing now mercilessly
Upon the frame of cracking bones,
Brittle from battle,

Wounds come and gone,
Healed to help remind
That time washes nothing,

But simply dulls the pain;
And the facts remain—

Carried by the camera,
Clicking constantly
Frame by frame,
Every detail our actions portrayed.

Nothing is sacred
To ourselves,
As even we escape into others,

In some kind of selfless slumber.
But always we must come back,
And that is the burden we attack.

In the relations of labor
And in the parameters of play,
Even in the sleep of dreams, some say.

But enough already;
This night belongs
To the grasshopper,

Who I now study
And who
Cocks his head

And looks back
As if to ask,
What is there to comprehend?

Passing over the Mad River Bridge

Reading, between drizzle,
A tiny, metallic green sign
Bolted to a metal stake:
The name of the river
Running under the bridge.

At 70 miles an hour,
You get to look just long enough
To see a large tree branch in the middle,
Rocking with the water's rhythm,
          Or so it appears.
For at this speed,
It could be standing still.

The water looks quite docile
On most days when I pass.
A great place to cast a fly
And bring lunch to shore,
Take a canoe or kayak through
The tunnel of trees.

I've seen this water sparkle in the sun,
Freeze to a stoic stillness in the cold,
But what exactly is mad about it,
I do not know.

For it looks not like a river,
But a pleasant stream
Big enough for abridge,
Small enough to skip a rock across.
Which makes me think

Of all the times I've driven over it.
I should one day stop
And walk to the water's edge,
Maybe disappear
Into its tranquil, melancholy, meandering flow
And come back with stories people ought to know,

Especially folks like myself,
Who pass daily with but a glance
And a chuckle
At what is deemed
A mad river.

December Day

Slowly afternoon
Makes evening;

      It is the color
      Before night.

Regrets   begin here

What was intended
Was this morning

But without warning
Here's what is now

Tea made from water
Boiled on the stove,

Season's gray sea
Above us   still and continuous,

Possibly   could the hours
Be made to last a bit more?

For they were made once before
To keep the light longer.

Warm belly
I feel calm and strong,

Content with the contexts
That what isn't   is okay,

Watching the dog running
Through the yards

Then back out to the open field
To his scolding master.

We have our own definitions,
And with that

I pardoned
My ambitions.

Anniversary of Infamy

Frozen grass
Stands gainst the curtain
Of iced trees.

Men
In florescent green jackets
Pick up trash
With mechanical arms
Along the highway's edge.

I pass their flashing pickup truck
Then cross the bridge,
Peeking at the river below,
And the four barges being towed.

A veteran talks of Pearl Harbor,
On NPR news,
I sip my café mocha,
Driving to Louisville,
Admiring the dashboard layout
Of my Japanese-made sedan.

My stomach then churns,
Caught now by the description
Of the bombing scene,
The gravelly emotion
Pouring through speakers.

"I was not born yet!"

I shout aloud,
As the reporter talks on,
Ignoring my pleas,
As I fight back tears.

The Distance Between

The sun is coming,
Peeking through the clouds
With winds of arctic air.

      Random drops of rain
      On the windshield,

Through which I look
Down a long highway
Lined with orange barrels
And green metal signs.

      Names of towns,
      Only known
      By white reflective letters.

Bridges built
At random intervals,

      Some to go over,
      Others
      To go under,

In this country
Between cities—

      One of which,
      I live in,

      The other

      Of which,
      I work in.

A melancholy landscape,
Serenaded by random songs,
Talk shows, and marching cars and trucks
Rolling to places,
Needed to be,
Registered with the plates of home.

I am anyone among everyone,
Moving in the ebb and flow
Of ambiguity's delirium
And the necessity of distance.

A New Technology

The tapping keys
Of the techno poet.

Short attention span.

No novels,
        Short stories,
        Essays,

Only poems,

        Short
        Very
        Short

        Poems.

Obsessive compulsive,
Everyday eccentric.

Cracked hands,
Over-washed,
Pounding away,   words

Conveyed as art,
        Truly therapy.

Little poems,
        A digital dream.

Errors deleted,
        They were never made.

Typewriters,
Pens,
          Their evident errors.

No one has to know
How long it took
To compose
A few lines,

Sometimes
In rhyme,
Others free

A   mystery,
    Perfect
A   Poem.

This Is Kite Weather

This is kite weather,
So the trees tell me.

Upon the hilltop,
I climb

And harness the water's breath
From the reservoir below.

To set flight
Plastic sticks and paper,

From which will ripple,
A melody of trance-like proportions,

Sending me into a catatonic state
Of thoughtless bliss.

Watch,
Listen,

And hold the string,
      Invisible.

Until it becomes grounded,
In the grasp of my fingers.

A conductor,
I shall linger about the day.

Until those rolling thunder clouds,
Come upon me to pronounce my awakening.

Thus by then,
My art will have been acted.

Midnight Poetics

I.

A page of paper sky,
What have I to deny?

Rhetoric's twilight,
Tonight, I just might …

       but never have the courage

Oh!
To be forthright … I could,

Never mind myself
So much as I do.

II.

God's mountains made for climbing.

       Clouds,

Cotton candy for the hands
To sift through
And touch Heaven.

III.

Sweet syllables
Rolling across the table.

I saw the dog jump
When the pen hit the floor—

A hilarious uproar,

A cruel thing.

Again

What I had
Forgotten

Has come
To be remembered

Under the solitary
Lamppost

In an umbrella
Of light

In which
I stand

Daring myself
To step out

Into the abyss
And forget

Again.

Before Bed

When I should have been in bed,
I stayed up reading poetry
And attempted to write my own.
I erased it all off the computer screen,
And that is the beauty of the delete button

      As if nothing was.

I walk upstairs with the rhythms of words
Pulsating through my head against eyes heavy,
Open the fridge and pour a glass of milk,
And I take it with me to the front porch.
Slowly sipping it down on the rocker,
I watch the full moon weave in and out of clouds.

A soothing glow the moon casts
To a world of noisy critters
Heard but not seen;
It is as vivid as a dream.

My bare feet keep me gently rocking,
And I might find myself soon asleep outside
To wake damp with the dew of this cool night,
Which causes the hair on my arms to stand up.

I only meant to be out here for a few minutes,
But the lingering lines of false poems keep me awake,
At least enough to finish the glass of milk
And sit rocking and breathing in steady harmony,
As if I was a Buddhist monk in a rocking mantra.

Maybe I am,
For I've shaved my head and relinquished
Many of my wears to the Goodwill drop box
And am draped in my robe watching faint breaths,

      Form and fade,
      Form and fade.

I have eyes open
But they no longer see.
Instead they pass off the night to the ears,
Which listen to the sound of the midnight moon,
Casting over the earth in a succulent glow
That takes everything there is to know
And buries it in the sound of tiny creatures,
Which make not noise
But melody of the midnight moon.

The Danger of Dreams

How the sun bleeds through the blinds,
The dog's tail thumps on the bed like a bass drum,
Tired bones intertwined,
Like branches amassed on the forest floor.

We knew the night
And carried the remains in our eyes,
Shared now in the whispers
Of a day not yet begun.

She speaks to me sweetly
And says,

> *Never do that again,*

> *Never let me go.*

How am I to know the actions of the unconscious?
Scrupulous and devious yet sweetly erotic,
I was not so much alive as I was comatose to my own devices.

Seeking not to hurt,
But to understand the kaleidoscope of living,
Turning in the cacophony of light in the night,
Ruminations of rumors and rambling theories.

The sheer drama of everything that I didn't know
Now coming to fruition, and so begins my act of contrition.
Thinking fast through what I could have done and said,
That now makes me fearful to lie in my own bed.

By Definition

I come looking,
      Again.
For what?
I know not.
But expect it
To come pouring
Out of my head,
As if it were a faucet
Of spiritual water
To grace me with
The strength to walk
Like a man should,
      And talk
Like a man should.

I don't beat women,
And drinking for debauchery,
Is not my thing.
Call me crazy,
Call me strange,
Call me that lonely man
Living in an apartment,
Who comes out only
To walk his dog,
      Rain or shine.
I did so in a snow storm,
And peed along with the dog,
      Made yellow snow,
      In weather ten below.

Yes, that is what I've become,
Before my days,
Before what hair is left on my head,
Turns gray.
I am the stoic who sits
And writes random words,
Searching the same way,
Every day for a cure.
Yes, insanity's definition is I,
      And it ain't so bad.

A Final Bow

Friday night in Chicago,
Watching love's naked sleep,
Keeping tabs on my thoughts' sound,
Loitering around against demands,
Drunk ecstasy in twilight's gleam.
My heavy-handed golden streams
Keep me real enough to stand stoic,
A street corner poet,
Silently acting out his art,
Philosophically spilling pieces of the heart,
Tainted and burned,
Tenderly healed,
Hardened and real.
I keep faith to make believe my ghost
Keeps walking into walls
And not so much through the parameters
Of parallel paradigms,
Design to impact the future form.
Retrospective vantage points,
The sun's set anoints the night's turn,
Masses marching, doctored up
For entrapment.
A game to play for some, for one night
And others keep for life.
How about it?
        Husband/wife

Does the dance make tribal romance?
Or does this playoff make one gay,
In the face of the world?
A finger of the middle index,
Pointing to God as the only judge and jury.
Therefore, bring forth your fury and know,
That whatever stings the skin cannot break within
The man/woman who stands affirmed.
Politicians, keep your lessons learned
And flop and flip about all you like,
As the money machine pours out your doctrine
While the masses parade about satiated by their choice,
Because it could be worse
And because it is as good as it gets.
For everybody knows king's rule in parades,
But the masses dictate ultimately their charades,
As political pawns are they who take harm
To foreign lands with the demands of but a few,
Who sing in suits and hide in threats.
They walk nowhere, never secured
By microphoned thugs
Who never break their lips to speak.
For they've been lobotomized in their tracks,
Programmed to search and react to attack,
The pauper's aggressive stance,
Because they believe the romance.
Of life lived in the liberty of a statute's shadow,
As hope floats past the gates again,
Dying to give generations not so much
The ideals of a nation, but life
To the ones they procreated,
Who come together in cities built prestigious,
On crystal waters and mountain's covers,
Across a vast and stolen land.

And I wonder high up on the twenty-fourth floor,
Why I give a damn and why I don't.
My choice is in the living,
My placement random.
This night, the sirens,
Someone dying,
Someone born.
The planet smaller
The buildings taller,
But the sun stills sets in the west,
And the moon and stars come out,
If the clouds allow.
So the street musician collects his coins
And takes a final bow.

He Got Drunk

He got drunk
       To laugh.

Instead
       He cried,

Told the world
       He tried,

Threw down
       The bottle

To hear it break,
       Told the world

This is the sound
       His heart makes.

Pouring

There are things to complain about,
But why bother tonight?
Nobody is here to listen;
So would I be,
That proverbial tree,
Fallen in the mysterious sea?

      Any sound,
      Anywhere,
      Anyone?

Anonymous night,
Sipping green tea, steaming my glasses,
Smudged already by clumsy fingers,
Correcting their stance on my face,
While maintaining focus to the screen.
I've traded work for joy,
And words are born.

Nothing much matters right now.
Clothes in the dryer tumbling
And full now, my belly no longer rumbling.
Kerouac on the desk, halfway read poetry,
My patron saint of sorts to this art.

What is the matter with me?
Nothing … I think … but that is my problem.
Sleep comes creeping, but my thoughts keep seeping,
Into every nook and cranny of my cranium,
Painting quite a conundrum of cacophonic space,
Nothing static … it all zips around until fingers pound
Each and every key lettered in black and white.

Goodnight I write,
Over and over … again,
Goodnight.

A Predetermined Dawn

A predetermined dawn,
Brings forth a tired and tried yawn,
For what sings the songs of so many,
Like the dreams that come a plenty
In visions the screens play.
Be it the television … computer,
Or the infinite other ways
That have come to fill our days,
So we won't have to.

Do you dream anymore?
And if so what color?
Do you have a musical score?

I dream … and dream often,
But wonder what matters I hold,
To sway … swoon … and seduce,
In order to produce such illuminate triumphs
And build the ego of myself,
A piece of integrity to last a legacy.

I wander roads,
Walk till the body aches,
From my heart down to my toes
And so my story builds and grows,
Playing characters to everyone I know,
Often sitting beneath the stars,
Wondering just how far
One must travel to solve this riddle
While often asking rhetorically to the night
Why must I run … to be someone …?

But only the heavy echo of the voice I know
So then I look to the next city light's glow.

Love City

"Because,"

        He said.

Staring into
His bottle of beer.

She waited
And never knew
The time
His watch read.

        He never buttoned his cuffs;

Then it rained.

City lights,
Muddled sparkles,

The empty noise of a crowd,
A puddle where toes drown.

Love,   sweet,   love,

Once,

        Never,

                But again,

Shall come about
To those

      Who

Wish
Want
And continue,

To ride in taxies,

      Alone.

Damp Day Rises

Damp day rises,
And the dogs walk their masters,

Clouds a seamless quilt,
Concrete and what recedes   drying

What creatures live beneath the bushes
In a vast network beyond the eye.

        Do not deny   they exist,

Like so much else
Without seeing
                Hearing
                    Believing.

Content in the context of duty,
Procreate not to exterminate,

Survival a trial of the day
As the machines come and dig out the clay:

Ants,
Worms,
And all things small

Devoured into the bucket of steel teeth
        Because we're bigger
        Because they're smaller.

Insignificance,
Not the size of existence,

Beauty beyond the eye
And often the mind,
A reason and purpose   for all.

And on my path,
I walk the sidewalk
Careful to step over and around
Ants and worms escaping

Saturated ground.

TWO

Conkle's Hollow

I walked
Above trees.

Flying
I was not.

Climbing
A staircase,

I was
Building muscle,

Muttering prayers,
Declaring myself wild,

Laughing,
At the modern world.

Blinded
By the sun,

Staring it
In the eye,

It had made me
Cry,

Though I was not
Sad.

But sweating
Out a poison,

With a grin
So wide

It could swallow
The sky.

Tree Houses

Getting ready for work
In the bathroom,
I brush my teeth
And glance out the window

To the woods out back
The trees standing naked,
Stoic statutes in the cold,
Their arms reaching out
To embrace the sun
And its elusive warmth.

I spit out
A gob of toothpaste,
Rinse off my brush,
My teeth shiny and new.
Again I peek out the window

To notice some trees hold nests,
Many more than I would have guessed,
An entire community in the branches
High above the earth,

Never noticed before
With all the leaves.
            Things taken for granted,
                    Bird's song missed
                    When they are gone.

Never thought much
About their homes.
I see now their sturdy structures
Empty in the trees,
Awaiting their return.

It won't be long,
Well, six weeks
According to the groundhog,
But what does he know?
Can he build a home in trees?

Through Night Skies

The glow of city lights
     On my right,

Stars of the country
     On my left.

My path,
Is that of the middle,

Paved through the twilight,
Of what is neither

Fiction nor fact,
But opposite

As I come back.

Two Poems

That silver moon,
A nail of a finger unseen,

The tip
Of a dream.

**

Outside, the stars
At eye level

And to catch one
In your hand

Tickles
Just a bit.

Wind in the Eye

Wind in the eye;
> Strange thing to brush away with the hand.

> As if it were a fly.

As if

Such things were dreams,
Flooding a vision vital,

For seeing sound,
Buzzing endlessly in the ear.

Such a quick and queer reaction,
To nothing's sound.

Under

The railing,
Of peeling paint,

Connecting to
The corner post

Holding the vacant
Robin's nest

Are the hornets,
Building,

Upside down,
In serious silent sound.

The Bee

In frozen peace
And prayerful pose,

Lying on the sidewalk,
A perfect site

To gently take
And hold and show

My son the wonders,
Of nature's little workers,

On the tip of fingers,
In close study to the eye.

But to the wind,
It can no longer fly,

So to the earth returned,
Life beyond sky.

Then questions come
To wondering why.

A father,
I gently try …

Strange Tree

A cell phone tower
In a forest on top of a hill.

May believe itself
To be a tree,

But it lacks
Branches, bark

And the nests
Of birds.

A flashing strobe,
Its peak,

Imposing a stoic stance
Of alien proportions,

Interrupting
A wilderness romance.

Half Moon

Two dogs bark,
Off in the random dark.

Their echoes ride the wind,
Carrying prayers within

For ears to drink
And minds to think,

That the half moon in the sky
May be God's winking eye.

Bullfrog Pond

What are not seen,
Are the frogs heard,

Their ripples evidence
Of where they never were.

After the Rain

Canadian Geese
Play in the field,
Where water
Has gathered
To look like a pond.

They splash
And nibble at their wings,
Squawking occasionally at another,
But they do not swim,

For the water is shallow
And from the rain.
But still they remain,
Acting as if it is deep enough
And their landing here
Was no mistake.

Windless Day

No windmill
On a steel frame

Welded together,
For one to stand.

Instead,
A television antenna,

Pointed
To the best reception

Over
A spent land.

A Walk at Dusk

A walk at dusk,
With my dog,
Under the streetlamp's
Luminescent glow.

Losing count
Of walnut-sized shadows
Of toads

Waiting still,
On the sidewalks
For us to pass,

In order
To disappear
Into night's
Cool, mysterious grass.

A Shade in Trees

Still the trees,
      Naked,
Their clothes
The carpet
Of leaves,

Which crunches
Under the weight
Of every step.

Until
I come across
A tree fallen,
Lying horizontal
In my path.

I climb upon it,
Stand up to see
That no taller am I,
Compared
To those around.

Even those lying
Sideways,
Have branches
Rising above me
In the canopy
Of veins against
The skin of sky.

But in shadows,
I am as tall as any,
Thanks to the
Slanted rays of the sun,

Blending in,
As if I
Have natural
Camouflage.

So I consider
This to be a place
For me to sway
In the wind
And stand stoic
In the heat.

Even if my shade
Is among the leaves,
It is a shade,
A shade in trees.

Daydream

Head full
Of trees,

I swallow
The clouds,

Let it rain
In my belly,

Until I glow
And sneeze out

      The sun.

The Moon Eye

The giant spooky orb,
Follows me all day,
And as the night approaches,
It begins to beam,
As if it caught sight
Of what I was trying to hide
And it has me cornered
In its diabolical scheme,
In which I would be exposed,
If only in my dreams.

But I sleep and sleep well,
No dreams.
And when out of bed,
I go to the window
And separate the blinds
To see if my moon companion
Is waiting stoically in the sky.

But I am denied.

The world a blanket
Of blinding snow,
And it continues to come down
Steady … silent … and purposeful—

Keeping me safe
Or
Keeping from me
The giant, haunting eye,
Sneaking a peek in day
Of what night would not say.

Oasis

The pond has come to be covered
By a green sludge of grass clippings
And the moss that grows on such surfaces.

The fountain still blossoms
Its crystal flowers
And the sound of their landing,
A steady and calming melody.

The red-tipped blackbirds
Chase through the cattails,
As the bullfrogs croak,
And the locust have arrived
To pass day to the cricket's night.

The moon is a sliver of itself,
A fingernail of God's hand
Pointing to direct the lost man,
Who squats by the water's edge.

He can't see his reflection here,
And that is the reason he is looking.
It is safe here among the so-called wild,
His back to the jungle of homes.

This oasis rescues him from every day,
Even in winter,
When all is a silent frozen gray.

Wind

Turbulence,
And the table breaks.

Fragments,
For a meal
Made of intentions.

**

Litter is
The branches
Of the old maple tree,

Shedding its shadow.

**

Waves or ripples,
This water is shallow,

Not to be construed
As hollow.

A giant gulp,
The earth can swallow,

     Gone.

Sky Looks Fierce

Thunder teases.

There has been lighting
On occasion.

Clouds intimidate.

Trees stand confusingly   still.

Though the earth
Grows a bit darker,

Only a few fat drops,
Nothing more.

Thunder continues,
Booming across the sky,

Teasing,
Knowing.

It can,
If it wants too.

And we
Can know not but when.

Watching the Dragon Fly

Dragon fly/water fly.
Good-bye my picture,
Rippling away to the clouds,
Coming over the rainfall.
Polka dots living in liquid,
      No squid below
This surface where the geese
Float carefree and en masse.

What if the crickets want
To dance to their own song,
While the stars shine their light
Upon the stage, before the lightning bugs
Begin their biopic play.
Wonder of such things,
      Big/small,
A crystal snow-globe ball,
How our universe may be,
Between the walls of the paranormal:

Preachers waxing poetic
On corners of big cities
And the meeting rooms of rural motels;
Musty odors;
Answers to it all in matters of time,
      Persistence/patience,
Revealing themselves so as not
To steal away the shine of mysteries
Made to keep intrigued the engine's fire,
For we all want to believe in something higher,
But for now I watch transfixed … the dragon fly.

Anonymous Autumn

Anonymous autumn
Comes falling in leaves.
Some lie in bed,
            Grieving.
Others make most,
As the holiday's host.
Still some chase ghosts,
Unsure of how
To shake their hands,
Invite upon the day conversation.

It could be because
Neither knows much of why
They are where they are,
Or how to overcome what
They've become,
Collecting like leaves
And swirling randomly
Through the air,
At the mercy of something,
None know for sure.

Blizzard

Buried in by snow,
What do I know
Of these hours?
In the solitude
That I've come
To have made
Mandatory to me.

Because I cannot
Go out and drive
In this blizzard,
My dreams broken
For a day,
And so I am left
To birth myself again

And come to terms
With the reality
That life is a series
Of fluid events.
And so, like water
That molds to the contours
Of which it passes over,
I too mold myself.

To the reality
That this day will be spent
Alone
And that I will celebrate
Thyself
And move to another day,
Dreams deferred
And the joys of a future
Anticipated.

Such visions are twice appreciated
When at first failed
They are dead.
But only when one is unwilling
Does faith carry a man,
And if you have but an ounce of such
What feats and joys will you know.

So grow, grow, grow
And watch it
Snow, snow, snow.

Morning Light

How the sun shines
Upon the hills rolling
From the eyes' gaze,

The haze of eternal light,
Casting shadows between
Branches on the cliff.

Where I wrangle over
The depths of trees
And the weight of flight.

To my own instincts
And conscious cares,
No fences there.

Thus I wander
Beyond and between
The sun and the moon,

How rapid such seasons,
Always needing reason,
So I touch sky and earth

Simultaneously.
Then nothing more,
But the robin's song.

Field of Play

In calm desolation,
Shadows spring,
Shapes between shapes,

Mimicking space,
A waste-less trace,
Game for a chase.

And when spoken to,
Back comes silence sincere,
But for the wind,

A soft roar
Of ocean invisible,
In language indivisible,

Between myself and I.

Water Moon

The water moon beams a living stillness
Through the trees of night
And beckons the chorus of twilight
To come and give day purpose,

So the living can break away
And rest for the episode
Of another cloud curtain rising,

While the lid of the inferno eye,
Beams wide beyond confines
Of this plastic terrarium,
To the dreams of the infinite.

As the million mirrors bounce back
The echo of light's transmission,
That we, too, send back as a glow.

I Stopped the Shovel

I stopped the shovel
And saw the worm
Moist in the soil
Far from the sun.

I pulled free
Everyone
But still I'm sure
I missed a few.

And their screams,
If worms did such,
Were buried
Beneath the tulips.

In Autumn

Disenchanted in the day,
Where wild
Fly the flurries.

**

The last leaves linger
On the tips of limbs,
Embracing sky.

**

Breath is seen,
From mouth,
From nose.

**

The chill comes in
To the bones
And down
To the toes.

**

Solitude is the window,
Staring across the field
To a rock standing stoic
And naked to it all.

**

The sky is shades of gray,
Rolling upon itself;

There will not be
A sunset.

**

Vacant homes in the trees,
No longer mysteries.

**

One more leaf falls,

Swaying
In the invisible current,

Spinning to a landing
Of sudden stillness.

**

Night is darker,

      Longer.

Stars aren't as often.

**

This wondrous world
Moves regardless.

In this first collection of poems, Eric Weiss explores humanity and nature as entities that are separate and, yet, completely of one essence. These poems take the reader on a kaleidoscopic ride of emotion and imagery in the landscape of our living, be that landscape the people we know or knew, the sights we see, or the lessons we must learn and teach. It is with simple and surreal honesty that these poems bring wonder and awe to the everyday occasions that we so ordinarily pass through; with such focus and profound thought, we will now walk with our senses in full bloom.

In Autumn stands as a reminder to us all of the conscious breaths of our being and wraps them into the art of our world, inspired by a grasshopper who ignites profound thought, the mystery of a river's name, the suspense the sky brings to the art a season paints.

Eric Weiss is a graduate of Otterbein College, where he received a bachelor's degree in English writing with a concentration on poetry. He was a member of the editorial board for the school literary journal, *Quiz and Quill*. His work has appeared in literary journals, and this is his first book. He currently works in publishing for Pearson and resides in Westerville, Ohio.

Key Words/Phrases:

This wondrous world, moves regardless.
Autumn
Eric Weiss
Sky
Emotion
Poems
Landscape
Grasshopper
Conscious
Down a Rural Road
Tracks of a Train
Mad River